Green Futures

In the series Agenda for the 21st Century

A Future for Socialism (Tony Benn)
Building the Global Village (Bruce Kent)
Green Futures (Sara Parkin)

Agenda for the 21st Century
Green Futures

by Sara Parkin

Do not borrow off the earth
for the earth will require its own back
with interest.

Swahili proverb

Fount

An Imprint of HarperCollins*Publishers*

First published in Great Britain in 1991 by Fount Paperbacks

Fount Paperbacks is an imprint of
HarperCollins*Religious*
Part of HarperCollins*Publishers*
77–85 Fulham Palace Road, London W6 8JB

Phototypeset by Intype, London
Printed and bound in Great Britain by HarperCollins
Manufacturing, Glasgow

A catalogue record for this book is available from the British
Library

For Colin and Douglas

Contents

Introduction

Man has hardly any troubles except those he has
given himself . . . It is only with great effort that
we have managed to make ourselves unhappy.
What is one to think of a relationship where the
reason of each individual dictates private maxims
directly contrary to those that public reason
preaches to the body of society, and in which
each one finds his profit in the unhappiness of
others?

Jean-Jacques Rousseau (1712–1778)

The start of a new millennium is a thoroughly
appropriate time to examine the predicament of
Human Beings plc. Some would say (and I am
amongst them) that an urgent review of the manner
in which we go about our business is way overdue
and that unless we radically alter our business practices we could be in danger of finding ourselves
bankrupt in more than a strictly economic sense.

Superficially,   the   balance   sheet   of   human

achievement appears impressive. Over the last century, the value of goods and services produced by us worldwide has grown twentyfold, our industrial production fiftyfold. Over the same period the world's food production has grown at a similarly impressive pace. Sophisticated communications systems now circle the world, making it possible for us to witness history as it happens. These achievements and the technological developments which made them possible are trumpeted as a matter of celebration.

Unfortunately, the progress they are thought to represent has turned out to be an illusion. As Lester Brown of the Worldwatch Institute in Washington has pointed out, the price of today's idea of progress *since 1950 alone* has been one fifth of the world's topsoil, one fifth of the world's tropical rainforest and the loss of tens of thousands of plant and animal species. And still the bills are coming as we discover levels of water and atmospheric pollution so extensive that climatic stability is imperilled. (BROWN 1990)

Economists may well say the world has become a much wealthier place over the last 100 years, but ecologists insist we are living beyond our means: they fear we have already entered a new era of 'uneconomic growth', one which impoverishes rather than enriches. (DALY & COBB 1989)

How has this happened? The blame for global climatic instability can hardly be attributed to 11 years of Mrs Thatcher's rule in the UK or even to 70-plus years of Communism. In Poland 65% of the river water is so corrosive that it is unfit for even industrial use, but the annual average concen-

trations of sulphur dioxide are higher in London
than they are in Warsaw. Even with a massive
increase in world production of food, around 850
million people live on the third of the world's land
which is threatened by desertification. For all their
wealth, over 40% of the people living in the 24
countries of the Organization for Economic Cooperation and Development (OECD) discharge their
sewage untreated into the seas and waterways. As
innumerable reports confirm, all over the world,
regardless of their household income or the ideologies of their governments, people are increasingly
exposed to levels of environmental degradation and
air, water and food pollution which are a danger
to human health. (OECD 1990 (a); UNEP 1990;
BRUNTLAND 1987; LEAN 1990)

No, environmental destruction which is so wide-
spread that it has destabilized climate on a global
scale cannot be merely a recent stumble on the
otherwise smooth path of human civilization.
Something more profound must be wrong with the
notions of progress and success we have chosen
for our species.

The unprecedented activity leading up to the
UN Conference on Environment and Development, due to be held in Brazil in June 1992, shows
that governments are at last beginning to understand this. In Brazil, for the first time in history,
representatives of every nation in the world will
meet to discuss "our common future". Three critical conventions are being prepared. One on greenhouse gas emissions, one on tropical rainforests
and one on biological diversity. However, it is also
obvious that governments are a long way from

understanding the practical steps they will have to take to fulfil any serious obligations such conventions may impose. Hope amongst them that slight adjustments to the business activities of Human Beings plc are all that will be necessary is to be found in equally large proportions to the fear that radical change will be required. A coherent plan is nowhere to be seen.

Any agenda designed to get us through the next 100 years will therefore have to be a very special one. It will have to address the grave environmental problems which threaten to destabilize every human project, whether it be feeding ourselves or struggling with economic systems which appear to have a life of their own. It will also have to recognize the huge potential for wrong decision-making that affects panicky governments under the pressure of immediate problems. But just as importantly, the agenda will have to be influenced as much by what has gone before as by what it is supposed to anticipate. If we are to avoid repeating the past errors which have brought us to our present dilemma, then we've got to recognize where we made them in the first place. Green futures sit squarely on a re-think about the past.

Chapter 1
Getting It Into Perspective

We have to steer between the danger of a dead antiquarianism, which enjoys the illusion that we can approach the past without preconceptions, and that other danger . . . of believing that the whole point of the past is that it should culminate with us.

Alisdair McIntyre, *A Short History of Ethics*, 1967

The end of a century is generally a comfortable, jolly occasion when the exciting achievements and events of the past 100 years are celebrated.

For example, at the end of the last century there were around 1,335 million people in the world. Some of them will have reflected on things as varied as the French Revolution, George Stevenson's locomotive, the publication of *The Communist Manifesto*, the American Civil War, Stanley explor-

ing the African Congo and the invention of the
telephone, zip fasteners and Coca Cola.

But the turning of millennia prompts a more
sweeping survey of history and of the cycles in the
affairs of human beings. This is usually a much
less comfortable experience. While one can *imagine*
100 years, and even meet people who live that long,
1,000 years is a *very* long time indeed. Examining
our progress through such a vast period of time
can be humbling, because, alongside our potential
to create great beauty and do great good, it reveals
just how deep are the depths to which we can
fall. Wars are, at most, counted in decades (the
Hundred Years War being in reality a spasmodic
rather than a continual affair), but in 1,000 years
empires have time to rise and fall and golden ages
have time to turn into dark ages. For this reason,
the turning of millennia tends to invoke gloom.
However big our ego as a species might be, behind
it lies the persistent human dread of failure and
loss of control.

... Spiritually

Around the time Jesus Christ was born most of the
many cults which flourished in what was to become
Europe sprang from a disillusionment with the
material world and dissatisfaction with the old
gods. As the beleaguered and 'insignificant backwater' of western Christendom emerged from the
dark ages, 1,000 years later, many believed the end
of the world was nigh, maybe because of the pas-
sage in the book of Revelation which announced
that 'when the thousand years are expired, Satan

shall be loosed out of his prison ... [to] go out to deceive the nations which are in the four quarters of the earth'.[1]

Today, as we approach the end of another 1,000-year period, it seems certain we are in for a similarly gloomy appraisal of our history and our future, apparently with more reason than ever before. Our physical relationship and our spiritual relationship with the earth seem to be in an equally parlous state. Many people feel today (as our ancestors felt in their way 1,000 and 2,000 years ago) that the 'old gods' no longer satisfy our spiritual needs, and that the environment, instead of giving pleasure and enhancing our lives, is increasingly threatening.

Such feelings are also being expressed by practitioners of Christianity – the cult which so captured the imagination of people 2000 years ago that it became a glue strong enough to bond together the western European empire even as it emerged from the fragmented dark ages. Sean McDonagh, a Catholic theologian and missionary, puts it like this:

> ... since the enlightenment period, Christians have no longer possessed a comprehensive *story of the universe* to guide them in their relationship with the Earth. This lacuna is particularly tragic as it coincided with the aggressive, exploitative expansion of western colonialism and the increased power of modern technology to repossess, and in many ways destroy, the natural world.
>
> [If] the spiritual disciplines which, when taken

together, inspire the adherents to live out their lives in accordance with the vision, ideals and norms which the religious tradition embraces . . . become lopsided, focused only on selective, peripheral elements within the tradition, or if they distort the truth that must be lived, then the spiritual energies of the faithful are misdirected and can often be quite destructive. (McDONAGH 1986)

. . . Demographically

One of the most startling features of the last 2,000 years is how many more people there are to look back on history. When Christ was born, there were only about 170 million people in the whole world; 1,000 years later, world population had not even doubled and stood at around 265 million.

By the year 2000, however, some 6,300 million people will be living on earth. That is nearly 25 times more than at the end of the last millennium, and five times more than at the end of the last century. Moreover, unless these growth rates are reversed, or at least slowed down, by the end of the 21st century world population could be nearly 14,000 million. To put these numbers in context, it is worth remembering that land makes up only 30% of the earth's surface. Of that only some 1,500 million hectares are fairly easy to cultivate and most of them are already in use. (LEAN 1990)

... Historically

Until half-way through the present millennium, history moved relatively slowly. The world knew a myriad of contrasting human cultures, with the majority of them, including the Chinese, Indian, western European and Islamic civilizations, for the most part unfolding independently of one another. Although they were very different traditions, in one respect they were alike: all were based on subsistence agriculture and relied on wind, running water and animal or human muscles as sources of energy. For a long time no one culture had the power to overwhelm the others.[2]

Then from 1500 onwards history began to gather speed for a final dash towards the 21st century. And the story of this period has been unequivocally a European one. Out of what had become a barbaric and insignificant backwater grew a culture and a power that was to dominate the world in a stunningly short period of time. So great was its success that all the most powerful institutions which govern world affairs today are influenced by traditions, values and beliefs which have been forged in western Europe. The World Bank, for example, is not known for its commitment to Buddhist economics. Nor is NATO famous for its interest in Gandhian methods of non-violent conflict resolution (nor was the Warsaw Pact, for that matter). Of the countries in the Organization of Economic Cooperation and Development (OECD), which represent only 16% of the world's population but which generate 76% of its trade and account for 50% of its energy use,

only Turkey and Japan are not predominantly
Christian.

... Scientifically

Although China developed movable type for printing (and many other innovations) long before the
Europeans did, it was in Europe that the invention
of printing presses stimulated the greatest change.
The ferment of scholarship which the printed word
permitted did much to underpin what history has
recorded as revolutionary changes in the way we
think about the world and about our own power as
human beings.

The starting date for what is known variously as
'the scientific revolution', 'the enlightenment' or
'the age of reason' is difficult to pinpoint. However,
a reasonable date for our purposes is 1543. This
was the year Nicholas Copernicus published his
mathematical evidence that the earth revolved
round the sun and not, as was commonly believed
at the time, vice versa. A short time later, helped
by the telescope which he had built, Galileo was
able to confirm these calculations. However, in
those days such discoveries were so controversial
that Copernicus was careful not to publish until
shortly before he died, and Galileo actually went
to prison as a result of his work. Not only was the
earth being ousted from its position of the centre
of the universe, but the whole cosmic arrangement
was being reduced to a collection of mathematical
formulae. The Church in particular, as supreme
guardian of faith and scholarship, was less than
happy to find God cast in the role of the Chief

Mechanic instead of that of the Mystical Creator of the universe.

Nevertheless, the notion of the world working to exact mathematical laws was subsequently developed by people like Isaac Newton and was soon widely accepted. Even the religious dilemma of God's precise role in creation was neatly resolved when a French philosopher, René Descartes, said there was nothing in the mind (by which he meant the spirit) that belonged to the body (by which he meant the material world). In effect, Descartes made it legitimate for scientists to reduce the material universe to the equivalent of a collection of nuts and bolts. God could remain the creator of all the bits and pieces, with his mystery manifest in the power of the human mind to reason and thereby work out how all the bits and pieces fitted together.

Without a doubt, this period was tremendously exciting. Natural phenomena like the movements of the planets, gravity, tidal flows, the behaviour of solids, liquids, gases, heat and sound, could all be explained in precise mathematical terms. In turn these discoveries could be translated into human creations. We became technologically skilled enough to emulate nature with machines of our own making. In what was the biological equivalent of a microsecond, we were able to evolve machines which went faster than sound and higher than any bird. Human beings managed to do what no other species could do: they shook off the major constraint of evolution – its slowness.

Not surprisingly, this made us a super-confident species. With our ingenuity, our enterprise, our innovation, we felt we could go anywhere, and do anything. And we did. Those 6,300 million people looking back on the 20th century will be considering events like the first powered airplane flight, the manufacture of the first Model T Ford car, the rise and fall of the Russian Empire, two World Wars, the advent of penicillin, AIDS, nuclear weapons, razor blades and frozen food, Mao Tse-Tung's Long March, the growth of UN membership from 50 to 160 countries, and Neil Armstrong's first steps on the moon.

However, in the year 2000, as in 1900, 1800 and 1000, it will be only a small proportion of the world's people who will be able to indulge in historical reflections such as these. The main concern of most people will be what it always has been – little more than their immediate condition. Technology may have advanced so quickly that only a century separates the completion of the American transcontinental railway and the sending of a man to a moon, but it still serves only a fraction of the world's citizens.

Despite the massive growth in economic wealth over the last 100 years, 60% of the world's people still live in countries in which the annual income per person is under $2,000 (BROWN 1991). Furthermore, *within the last decade* whole continents, for the first time in modern history, began to register a drop in average annual income per person. And, of course, behind all such averages lies the fact that the majority of people are below rather than above them. There may be an estimated 50 billion books in the world, but they are accessible to a minority rather than a majority of people. More than one quarter of the world's adult population, 98% of them living in the poorest countries, are unable even to read or write. (LEAN 1990)

... Ecologically

Warnings and worries about the degradation of our natural environment have been sounded through-out recorded history in most cultures. Even Plato wrote of the effects of deforestation. After all, a fairly predictable climate and a reasonably safe environment are the most fundamental human needs of all. The 19th-century traveller G. P. Marsh made the following observations:

> Almost every narrative of travel in those coun-tries which were the earliest seats of civilization, contains evidence of the truth of these general statements ... With the extirpation of the forest, all is changed ... climate becomes excessive ... The precipitation becomes as irregular as the temperature ... The face of the earth is no longer a sponge ... It appears then, that the fairest and fruitfullest provinces of the Roman Empire ... are now completely exhausted of their fertility, or so diminished in productiveness, as, with the exception of a few favoured oases that have escaped the general ruin, to be no longer capable of affording sustenance to civili-zed man.[3]

In each age contradictory attitudes to nature are evident. More often than not, the notion of the earth as a bountiful mother is balanced by another vision of nature as capricious, or even vengeful.

The Greek goddess Gaia may have epitomized benign nature, but her son Zeus often deployed extreme meteorological special effects. Similarly, the Old Testament God was a bountiful creator but was also prone to using natural disasters like floods or swarms of locusts as punishments.

As day-to-day living has never been a risk-free venture for human beings, our ambivalence towards nature is understandable. From our cave days onwards, to a great extent our development patterns have been geared (so we imagined) to minimizing those risks. We have sought security by either defending ourselves from risk or trying to reduce the threat it has posed. For example, from the beginning human beings have built themselves protection from adverse weather conditions and have laid in stores against shortages of vital supplies. Taking out insurance policies on our homes or the life of the family bread-winner is simply a modern version of that basic instinct to secure ourselves against risk. We have also waged a long struggle to replace the dangerously unpredictable wilderness with a safe and orderly garden. The Romans saw it as a straightforward engineering problem:

> We enjoy the mountains and the plains. The rivers are ours. We sow the seed and plant the trees. We fertilize the earth ... We stop, direct, and turn the rivers: in short by our hands we endeavour, by our various operations in this world, to make, as it were, another Nature.[4]

Our manicured parks and our managerial approach to the countryside and agriculture show that this attitude is alive and well today. There may be a welcome move towards sowing wild-flower verges, but generally speaking, weeds and jungles are out and regimented municipal flowerbeds are in.

However, it was not until we had gained the powers made possible by the industrial revolution that we could really *fight* the known and unknown risks of nature. We set out to conquer nature not only with our machines (which surpassed many of her powers) but also by knowing the details of her most intimate workings. Francis Bacon, when he was developing his methods of scientific experimentation in the middle of this millennium, quite openly spoke of subjugating the wildness of the natural world to the discipline of the human will. Nature was to be 'bound into service' and made our 'slave'. The scientist would 'torture nature's secrets from her' for the benefit of mankind.[5]

Not surprisingly (particularly in response to such violent language), women writers like Caroline Merchant have commented on the parallels which exist between men's ambivalent relationship with nature and their relationship with women.

Merchant also points out that, once it became commonplace to view the living world in a purely mathematical and mechanistic light rather than as a sometimes caring, sometimes chastizing mother, we lost many of our earlier inhibitions about violating the earth.

> The image of the earth as a living organism and nurturing mother had served as a cultural constraint restricting the actions of human beings . . . As long as the earth was considered

to be alive and sensitive, it could be considered a breach of human ethical behaviour to carry out destructive acts against it.[6]

The seal on our current view of the world was thereby set by what Descartes called the 'marvellous science'. By rejecting 'all knowledge which is merely probable' and judging 'only those things . . . which are perfectly known and about which there can be no doubts' to be real, the nagging human fear of losing control and failing could be overcome. Scientific endeavour from thenceforth was devoted to the pursuit of complete knowledge of nature and thereby total domination and control of her. The goal for humankind was to achieve mastery of the universe.

But because 'marvellous science' required the exclusion of all that could not be satisfactorily described numerically, scientific inquiry focused on the tiny particles – the atoms and the genes – which form the building blocks (the nuts and bolts) of nature. This sort of research certainly enabled us to build space rockets to take us into the universe, but by concentrating on things which could be 'perfectly known' (i.e. counted) we unfortunately neglected to study the 'big picture'. Few scientists studied the way the whole system of life worked.

As a consequence, we know relatively little about the apparently infinite (and therefore incomputable) number of *connections* between the myriad particles and systems in the natural world – all those *strands* in the web of life which make it at once strong and fragile. Our limited, mechanical way of seeing the world has simply not equipped us to understand how the different parts of the web of life relate to one another, and therefore how they might respond to varying degrees of damage.

So with the evidence of environmental damage on a global scale now pouring in, we find ourselves cast adrift from the scientific certainty with which we had conquered our fear of nature. What is happening now is beyond both the control of our technology and the limits of our understanding and knowledge. The quintessential example of our predicament in this new era of uncertainty is global warming.

There are more than 20 known feedbacks (connecting loops) which, in a warming world, can either amplify global warming (positive feedback) or dampen it (negative feedback). Of these, 14 are known to be or are strongly suspected to be positive if no precautionary action is taken and warming proceeds. However, only a few of these feedbacks are incorporated in the global climate models on which the scientists base their predictions about the speed and magnitude of global warming. Since there is a lack of detailed knowledge about these important connecting loops in the climate system, they cannot be quantified in models, said the 300 scientists reporting to the Intergovernmental Panel on Climate Change in June 1990. Nevertheless, these same scientists, backed by a huge number of their colleagues, made very clear their belief that it is 'likely' that the positive rather than the negative feedbacks will predominate. They urged a speedy global cut in the emissions of greenhouse gases caused by human activity, asking for at least a 60% drop in the production of long-lived gases (carbon dioxide, nitrous oxides, CFCs) and a 15–20% one for the shorter-lived gas methane. (LEGGETT in PARKIN 1991; HOUGHTON et al. 1990)

Governments were aghast. First, because politics and economics have developed along very much the same lines as has science, this lack of scientific certainty was irritating to say the least. For almost as long as the 'Baconian spirit' has been alive in science, a similar approach has been adopted by governments with respect to the analysis of social and economic activity. Policies, particularly economic ones, are largely determined by mathematical modelling which is supposed to mimic the real effects of policy in the outside world. Numerical, 'scientific' justification for action is the stuff of which modern governments are made.

Secondly, what if the scientists were largely correct? It is indeed exceptional for so many scientists to be in such agreement over anything, and here were hundreds of them, many in government posts, predicting a mean rise in global temperatures of 3°C and a mean sea-level rise of 65 cm over the next century. The risks of ignoring these predictions would therefore be enormous. But a worldwide 60% *decrease* in emissions of the main greenhouse gases! That implies an even larger percentage decrease on the part of the high-emitting countries, and therefore policies which do not fit at all easily with the current political agendas of the governments of most of those countries.

It is true that for a while now, governmental projects have been suffering from constraints which have increasingly been imposed by the environment. Not only do people not want to have chemi-

cal or waste disposal plants in their neighbour-
hoods, or to see yet another greenfield site go
under concrete, but they are also distressed by the
endless TV images of human misery at home and
on other continents. More and more difficult questions are being asked and, despite vigorous sear-
ches in their ideological holdalls, governments are
finding answers difficult to produce.

But now the prospect of massive numbers of
people having to move away from areas of failing
harvests or rising sea-levels on a global scale poses
problems which stump even the most imaginative
politician. The world struggled to deal with the
movement of 2 million or so Kurdish refugees, and
was overwhelmed by the tragedy of flood-stricken
Bangladesh and by the plight of the tens of millions
of starving people in sub-Saharan Africa. How on
earth will we cope with the hundreds of millions
of people who will be obliged to move if global
warming continues unchecked into the next century?

With such uncertainty surrounding the manner
and timing of climate change, taking a purely
defensive approach (like building sea defences)
would require enormous sums of money and would
involve immense planning difficulties. Similarly, to
concentrate on 'fighting back' with technological
wheezes (like spreading dust in the upper atmos-
phere to reflect the sunlight) would also be enormously expensive and would be even more specu-
lative. Not only that, but it would also take us
uncomfortably close to a final show-down between
ourselves and the forces of nature, which in our
heart of hearts we fear we cannot win. Ultimately,

however sophisticated our technology may be, it cannot hold back the sea or bring back lost topsoil.

Slowly, excruciatingly slowly, politicians are being forced to accept what the scientists are urging and many ordinary people know instinctively to be true – that is, that the only sensible way forward is to take *preventive* action and stop doing the things which are causing the problem. Instead of letting our historical ambivalence towards nature keep us trapped in our usual 'flight or fight' responses to fear and risk, the time seems ripe for investing our cash and ingenuity in a grand reconciliation between ourselves and nature.

However, considering such a step puts governments into an intensely uncomfortable position. It means acknowledging that there is something wrong with current notions of progress and success. This in turn cuts across the grain of thinking in every possible department – finance, industry, energy, agriculture and so on. It even undermines the basis on which world institutions, including the United Nations, were founded. Although he is probably not aware of it, to speak of making peace with nature, as Edouard Saoama, the Director General of the Food and Agriculture Organization did recently, is actually revolutionary talk.[7]

Chapter 2
Picking Up Positive Signals

An ethic, ecologically, is a limitation on freedom of action in the struggle for existence. An ethic, philosophically, is a differentiation of social from anti-social conduct. These are two definitions of one thing.

Aldo Leopold, *A Sand County Almanac*, 1948

Making peace with nature will mean admitting honestly that as a species we have so overstepped the limits of ecological balance that we have seriously damaged the web of life; while we may have genuinely thought we were diminishing the risks of living with nature, we seem instead to have amplified them. It will mean admitting that a full understanding of how the fabulously complex strands connect and interrelate is probably beyond our power, and that moving in with a technological repair kit is likely to make matters worse, not better.

It will also mean agreeing that the best move we can make now is to stop crashing about in the web and let nature do what it has been doing successfully for millions of years – that is, maintain a life-supporting environment. James Lovelock describes nature as:

> A complex entity involving the earth's biosphere, atmosphere, oceans and soil; the total constituting a feedback or cybernetic system which seeks an optimal physical and chemical environment for life on this planet. (LOVELOCK 1979)

We may call that complex entity nature, the earth, Gaia, the environment, whatever we like, but the messages it is sending could not be clearer. Its integrity – its well-being – is seriously threatened by our activities. However, because *our* well-being is intimately connected with that of the earth, getting our activities into harmony with the web of life is a prerequisite to a sustainable and satisfactory future.

Making those connections, starting to think of the relationships between ourselves and the natural world, is the first step in ecological thinking. So far this is territory on which only the Greens have dared to tread. By bringing together all the things we thought were separate – our minds and the material world around us, our spirituality and the mystery which makes the universe much larger and more powerful than the sum of its parts – Greens are crafting what commentators on the 21st century will surely look back on as a turning point in history.

Not surprisingly, dating the start of what may

become known as 'the green revolution' or 'the new enlightenment' or even 'the age of ecological reason' will probably be as hard to do as pinpointing the beginning of the scientific revolution set in train by Nicholas Copernicus. But the 'green revolution' is sure to be viewed as being just as important as (if not more important than) the Copernican one in deciding the destiny of human beings.

... Scientifically

Scientists themselves will perhaps date the green revolution from early this century, when physicists engaged in subatomic research first challenged the mechanical world-view of Newton and Descartes. Ironically, it was during the experiments which eventually led to the building of the first atom bomb (and which gave us the power to end all life) that a quite unexpected discovery was made. It had been expected that the research would show that atoms were solid, divisible particles, but instead they turned out to consist mostly of empty space, while their sub-particles appeared sometimes as matter, sometimes as waves, depending on how they were observed. Writing about this subatomic world, Niels Bohr, one of the scientists, noted: 'isolated material particles are abstractions, their properties being definable and observable only through their interaction with other systems'. The world was not a heap of nuts and bolts after all, but a dynamic set of relationships in which human beings played an active part. Another nuclear physicist, James Jeans, said 'the universe begins to look more like a great thought than like a great machine'. (CAPRA 1982)

Just as Copernicus and Galileo were accused of heresy because of their discoveries, so the discoveries of these 20th-century scientists produced a great shock. They themselves remember it as an intensely emotional, even an existential experience. Albert Einstein felt 'as if the ground had been pulled out from under [him], with no firm foundation to be seen anywhere'.

Moreover, because no atomic event could be predicted with certainty – only the likelihood of its happening could be predicted – one of the problems faced by the scientists involved in these experiments was that the language of certainty employed by classical physics was not adequate to describe their observations. At the subatomic level, matter did not exist at definite times in definite places, but rather had a 'tendency to exist'. Particles which were also waves at the same time had to be called 'probability waves'.

Climate scientists today, faced with the inability of their models to predict future events with absolute certainty, but obviously confident enough that global warming is happening to issue their predictions, must know exactly how Bohr and the others felt nearly 80 years ago. The language of scientific certainty has failed them on a global scale, just as it failed their colleagues at the subatomic level.

... Historically

It would seem, therefore, that life at every level, from the subatomic to the cosmic, is a long way from being the clock-like mechanism described by the scientists of the 16th century. Their assumption that if we could understand how the smallest cog or unit of life worked, we would be able to extrapolate this understanding to the whole of life, is obviously no longer tenable. The new view of the earth as a self-regulating organism more complex than we can imagine is far more in tune with the reality we find around us.

Actually, thinking of the world as *one* complex eco-system is not as new an idea as all that. In fact, only 50 years after the death of Isaac Newton, James Hutton, a Scottish physician turned farmer and natural philosopher, rejected the prevailing fashion for the microscope and declared that the earth was one 'macrocosm'. In 1795 he wrote:

> We live in a world where order everywhere prevails ... life is the final cause not only for the circulation of the blood but for the revolution of the globe ... Therefore the explanation, which is given of the different phenomena of the Earth, must be consistent with the actual constitution of this Earth as a living world, that is, a world maintaining a system of living animals and plants. (HUTTON 1795)

As history reveals, the idea did not catch on until somewhat later. Round about the time when physicists were discovering the subatomic world, a new generation of natural philosophers (called 'earth scientists' or 'biogeochemists') began to refine the notion of the earth as a biosphere. The term itself was first coined in 1875 by Eduard Suess, a Viennese geologist, and the concept was considerably expanded by a Russian, Vladimir Vernadsky, in the 1920s. (GRINVALD in PARKIN 1991)

But it was not until the space exploration programme provided that wonderful picture of the earth from space that we could truly believe in Hutton's notion of one living world. For ex-NASA scientist James Lovelock, as for many others, the technological achievements of the moon shots were secondary considerations:

> The real bonus has been that for the first time in human history we have had a chance to look at the Earth from space, and the information gained from seeing from the outside our azure-green planet in all its global beauty has given rise to a whole new set of questions and answers. (LOVELOCK 1979)

Despite the profound nature of these questions and answers, commentators tracing the roots of the modern green movement rarely trespass onto such metaphysical territory. They keep their feet firmly on the ground as they chronicle the history of environmentalism and the growth of environmental groups and legislation over the last 150 years or so.

The earliest stirrings of environmentalism were very much in the tradition of the scientific revolution. From the 16th century onwards the study and classification of animals and plants was not only a scientific passion but also a popular pastime.

The earliest groups to actually campaign for environmental protection or conservation grew up from the 1860s onwards, particularly in Britain and America. International organizations like UNESCO and the Worldwide Fund for Nature became popular somewhat later and governments agreed several multilateral treaties, though not all were implemented. Some even became known as 'sleeping conventions' because of the inability of signatory nations to either enforce or administer them. (McCORMICK 1989)

But for most people today, and I suspect for most future historians too, the birth of the modern green movement dates from the publication in 1962 of *Silent Spring*, Rachael Carson's devastating critique of the Unites States' chemical industry and its products. A best seller for many months, it brought home to many people the fact that there was a limit to the biosphere's power to tolerate unthinking human activity.

> We have allowed these chemicals to be used with little or no advance investigation of their effect on soil, water, wildlife, and man himself. Future generations are unlikely to condone our lack of prudent concern for the integrity of the natural world that supports all life. (CARSON 1962)

Silent Spring also provides a useful marker for reasons other than its massive impact on public perception. Although a Science Advisory Committee set up by President Kennedy vindicated everything Carson said, the chemical industry mounted a bitter and unscrupulous attack on her. Subsequently, however, the industry took more care to

organize itself in a way which allowed it to maintain
its activities while protecting itself from too close
scrutiny. Overall it was successful. It did improve
some of its practices, but usually only in the face
of legislation or public opprobrium, and it made a
particular effort to be at the heart of any decision-
making process which might affect it. For example,
the committees which advize the European Commission on standards for emissions of various
chemical substances include representatives from
the industry but no independent environmentalists.

Indeed, since *Silent Spring* was written, the
amount of synthetic organic chemicals produced
by the USA alone has increased fivefold – from 20
million or over 100 million tons per year. Worldwide some 70,000 chemicals are in everyday use.
Today, with several major accidents – like those at
Bhopal in India, Seveso in Italy and the Sandoz
plant in Switzerland – further destabilising public
confidence, the industry says it is developing 'safe'
chemicals, particularly for use in agriculture. However, many chemicals which were thought to be
safe back in 1962 have since proved to be harmful
and, even now, little or no research is being done
on the effect which 'cocktails' of chemicals may
have on the environment and human health. In
short, despite the alarm sounded by Rachel Carson,
little has changed. Indeed, the rate at which chemicals are being poured into the environment has
accelerated.

Sadly, the same trend is evident in many areas of
environmental concern. Over the last 20–25 years,
despite many international conferences, the setting
up of environmental agencies in over 130 countries,

the signing of more than 180 international agreements and the forming of several thousand nongovernmental environmental organizations, the net result has been an acceleration of environmental degradation. (McCORMICK 1989)

... Ecologically

Ten years after the publication of *Silent Spring*, the UN held a conference in Stockholm on the Human Environment. Delegates from 114 countries signed a declaration which said:

> To defend and improve the human environment for present and future generations has become an imperative goal for mankind – a goal to be pursued together with, and in harmony with, the established and fundamental goals of peace and of world-wide economic and social development.[8]

Much of the debate about the environment around the time of the Stockholm conference was concerned with 'limits to growth', or the problem of an essentially finite biosphere coping with an apparently infinitely growing human economy (i.e. a rapidly growing world population consuming a rapidly growing proportion of the world's resources and thereby causing a rapidly growing amount of degradation and pollution). The language of doom was frequently used. 'Mankind itself may stand on the brink of extinction', said Paul and Anne Erlich, authors of many books and articles on the subject. (see for example ERLICH & ERLICH 1987; 1990)

One of the most famous books of that period was *The Limits to Growth*, commissioned from the Massachusetts Institute of Technology by a group of concerned scientists, businessmen and politicians calling themselves the Club of Rome (MEADOWS et al 1972). They felt that catastrophic breakdown was inevitable by the end of the 20th century. Other books like *A Blueprint for Survival*, produced by the editors of the British magazine *The Ecologist*, and *Small is Beautiful* by the economist E. F. Schumacher echoed the same themes but tempered them with suggestions for political and economic changes by which catastrophe might be avoided. (THE ECOLOGIST 1972; SCHUMACHER 1973)

Although the oil crisis of 1973 seemed to confirm the warnings of these books, many of their precise predictions proved to be wrong. The environment and people's ability to adapt to events proved to be more resilient than imagined. The doom-sayers of the early 1970s may not have hit the bull's-eye with the dates and details of the final collapses and catastrophes, but their arrows were certainly aimed at the right target.

For example, Paul Erlich anticipated the collapse of the whaling industry by 1973. It did not collapse that year. However, provisional figures given in 1989 by the International Whaling Commission reveal that only about 10,000 sperm whales are left, while numbers of humpback whales are down from 200,000 to 4,000, those of fin whales are down from over 100,000 to around 2000 and those of blue whales are down from more than quarter of a million to around 500. (LEAN 1990) Whether exaggerated or underestimated, these figures seem to represent a collapse in the number of whales. Do we have to wait until the last whale is gone for the whaling industry to collapse?

In 1968 Erlich also forecast that the imbalance between human population and resources would lead to 50 million deaths through malnutrition per year by the end of the 1970s. He was wrong. That decade's rates of population growth slowed and food production increased. However, nowadays around 20 million people do die of starvation each year, and in 1991 it could well be more, with an estimated 30 million menaced by famine in sub-Saharan Africa. Furthermore, while the World Bank calculates that 1,000 million people (one fifth of the world's population) do not have enough food for productive activity at the moment, the graph of increased productivity for the main grains – corn, wheat and rice – has begun to level off and the populations of the countries where hunger is greatest are expected to double by around 2010 (WORLD BANK 1986; BROWN 1989). Whichever way you look at them these figures represent massive human misery. Do we have to wait until precisely the number of deaths anticipated by Erlich is reached before we accept his thesis?

Anyone would be forgiven for wondering if we really do have to wait for some so-far-undefined limit for whales, rainforests, starving people or levels of chemicals in our food to be passed before we truly believe the mountain of reports which warn that we are living far beyond the means of the planet. One of them was the first attempt by any

government to examine the relationships between
people, resources and the environment in the
future (GLOBAL 2000 1982). Commissioned by
President Carter, this report was completely shel-
ved by Ronald Reagan, despite its powerful open-
ing words which underlined how near the limits
we appeared to be:

> If present trends continue, the world in 2000
> will be more crowded, more polluted, less stable
> ecologically, and more vulnerable to disruption
> than the world we live in now. Serious stresses
> involving population, resources and environment
> are clearly visible ahead. Despite greater material
> output, the world's people will be poorer in many
> ways than they are today.
>
> For hundreds of millions of the desperately
> poor, the outlook for food and other necessities
> of life will be no better. For many it will be
> worse. Barring revolutionary advances in tech-
> nology, life for most people on earth will be more
> precarious in 2000 than it is now – unless the
> nations of the world act decisively to alter current
> trends.

Human economic activities have always
impinged on the environment (admittedly often in
ways we could not see or understand) but in the
1980s a new dimension was added – the state of
the environment was imposing increasing constraints on our economic activity. The era of 'uneconomic growth' had begun. Although the usual
economic indicators showed continued world pros-
perity, other indicators, human and environmental,
were suggesting a net drop in well-being.

In rich and poor countries alike, more and more people were dropping into poverty, and more and more people were complaining (and dying) because of environmental degradation and pollution. The decade saw images of millions suffering from starvation in Africa, of soup kitchens and cardboard cities in Washington and London, and of the wholesale collapse of the economies of the Warsaw Pact countries. It also saw huge changes in the dynamic of the world economy. For example, 1981 was the last year in which there was a net flow of aid, loans and investment from the rich countries to the poor ones. From 1982 onwards the direction of the flow reversed, so that now there is a net transfer of cash from the poor countries to the rich ones of around US $50,000 million per year. (GEORGE 1988)

Recognizing the deepening economic crisis, the UN General Assembly set up the World Commission on Environment and Development. The remit of the commission was to address the relationship between environment and development and come up with 'A global agenda for change' (BRUNDTLAND 1987). Explicit in the mandate of the commission was the need for:

significant changes in current approaches: changes in perspectives, attitudes and life styles; changes in certain critical policies and the ways in which they are formulated and applied; changes in the nature of cooperation between governments, business, science and people; changes in certain forms of international cooperation which have proved incapable of tackling many environment and development issues; changes, above all, in the level of understanding and commitment by people, organizations and governments.

Entitled *Our Common Future* but more generally referred to as the Brundtland Report after the Chair of the Commission, Mrs Gro Harlem Brundtland, Prime Minister of Norway, the report has been roundly (and rightly) criticized because, although it produced an impressive indictment of the failure of existing institutions to respond to the *causes* of the problems, it was self-contradictory in its own conclusion, which called for 'sustainable development' to be fuelled by increased economic growth. For development (or growth) as it is currently pursued in both rich and poor countries is exactly what is proving to be unsustainable.

Herman Daly and John Cobb wonder if Mrs Brundtland might be playing a very clever and ultimately subversive political game:

> One of the reasons for the unanimity of support given to the phrase, 'sustainable development' is precisely that it has been left rather vague – development is not distinguished from growth in the Brundtland Report, nor is there any distinction between strong and weak sustainability. (DALY & COBB 1989)

They point out that any government or institution attempting to pursue the report's definition of sustainable development (i.e. development that 'meets the needs of the present without compromising the ability of future generations to meet their own needs') will have to resolve two key questions. First, how do we distinguish a 'need' from an extravagant luxury or an impossible desire? For example, if a car each for 1 billion Chinese is a 'need' then sustainable development is impossible. Thus the whole question of *sufficiency* will have to be examined. Secondly, to leave uncompromized the ability of future generations to meet their own needs raises the tricky question about the *substitution* of natural capital with human-created capital. Can a theme park, for example, be a substitute to future generations for a forest or agricultural land in the same way as margarine is supposed to be an adequate substitute for butter? Examining the notions of sufficiency and substitution goes to the heart of present economic theory.

. . . Politically

During the 1970s and the 1980s a growing number of people became frustrated by the inability of governments to turn their words of concern about the environment into actions which would at least slow the rate of environmental and human degradation. They also began to discover just how close were the links of dependence between governments and the industries and institutions which bore the largest responsibility for making matters worse, not better.

For example, in the Australian island state of Tasmania a group of people led by Dr Richard Jones were concerned about the proposed flooding of Lake Pedder by a hydro-electric company. Obvious complicity over the scheme between the two main political parties and the company convinced Dr Jones and his colleagues that they would have to take their objection to the voters. They formed a party called the United Tasmania Group (UTG), which just missed winning a seat in the April 1972 Tasmanian state elections. Although the UTG failed to stop Lake Pedder being flooded, the experience the group gained helped them to stop a similar scheme for flooding the Franklin River (now a World Heritage Area). Eventually they won enough seats in the state parliament to hold the balance of power.

Although the primary goal of their foray into electoral politics was to protect Lake Pedder, the UTG understood not only the conflict between environmental protection and the economic development of Tasmania but also the compromized position of the politicians, which hampered their ability to make decisions in the best long-term interests of Tasmanians. It was therefore not by chance that the UTG included in its political programme *A New Ethic* which prompted the Tasmanian *Examiner* of 26th August 1976 to comment: 'Dr Jones' little party has produced more teasing relevant ideas for Tasmanians than all the other party policy writers put together.'

This search for new values in politics is echoed in the development of many of the world's green political parties. In 1972 the first nationwide green party in the world was founded in New Zealand. It was simply called Values, and one of its founders pointed out that many people were fed up with 'lying under the tap marked Labour, waiting for a drop of moral leadership'. The following year, what

was to become the UK Green Party was founded.
Long before Mrs Brundtland made the notion of
sustainability famous, the Green Party had focused
its programme on the four points that *A Blueprint
for Survival* offered as the 'principle conditions of
a stable society – one that to all intents and purposes can be sustained indefinitely while giving
optimum satisfaction to its members . . .

1. Minimum disruption of ecological processes,
2. Maximum conservation of materials and
   energy,
3. A population in which recruitment equals
   loss,
4. A social system in which individuals can
   enjoy, rather than feel restricted by the first
   three conditions.'

Around about the same time, a Jesuit priest in
Belgium was becoming disillusioned with present-
day Catholic teaching. He felt that three values
which had become dominant in society – rivalry,
consumption and competition – should be replaced
with the early Christian values of peace, frugality
and community. Out of the movement he started,
which was called *A*nders *Ga*an *Lev*en, meaning 'go
live differently', Agalev, the Flemish green party,
was founded. The Swedish green party, Miljöpartiet de Gröna (Environment Party – The Greens),
was founded under similar circumstances. A Lib-
eral member of the Swedish parliament, Per
Gahrton, left not only parliament but his party in
despair over the corruption and patronage which
dominated politics and made it difficult to put the
well-being of people and the environment above

the demands of narrow economic interests. He circulated a personal manifesto for a new party based on ecological ethics. From these beginnings Miljöpartiet developed, eventually winning 20 seats in the Swedish parliament. (PARKIN 1989)

Although not all green parties were founded on such strong ethical bases, many were. The most famous, the German party Die Grünen (The Greens), was, in fact, one of the few which were not. Although he received little publicity, the first Green to get into a national parliament was actually a Swiss, who won his seat in 1979. He was followed by 9 Belgian Greens in 1981 and then 27 German and 2 Finnish Greens in 1983. Today, Greens sit in 18 national parliaments around the world and are represented at some level of local government in almost every industrialized country. By any standards, this makes them the fastest-growing political force the world has ever seen. In contrast to the much-publicized travails of Die Grünen, the Greens in Switzerland, Belgium and Finland have increased their parliamentary representation over three general elections.

The great surge of popular and political interest in green ideas has not been restricted to the western world. In eastern Europe, environmental protest preceded the large demonstrations for democracy in most countries, with small but brave groups of people tackling their repressive governments over environmental problems. Probably the best known of these campaigns was in Hungary, where a group called Duna Kör (Blue Danube) fought strenuously against the damming of the Danube river. But others, like the Ecological Library in

East Germany, the Polish Ecological Club, Eco-glasnost in Bulgaria and Brontosaurus in Czecho-slovakia, also played key roles in the years and months before the final revolutions.

In northern India, the Chipko Andolan or 'Tree-Hugger Movement' grew up in the 1970s. Their slogan 'ecology is permanent economy' was inspired by the forests which provide them with almost all their needs – firewood, food, animal fodder and herbal cures and treatments. However, felling of the trees resulted in the soil being washed away by the rains. This made agriculture imposs-ible; moreover, sometimes whole villages were buried in mud-slides. The movement became world famous when its women members embraced trees to protect them from the bulldozers and chain-saws of commercial logging companies.

Also focusing on trees is the Green Belt Move-ment in Kenya, founded by Professor Wangari Maathai, Chair of The National Council of Women of Kenya, and run entirely by women. Its goal is to grow trees from local seeds and then transfer them to as many villages, schools and farms as possible. The women make a point of handing on not only forestry skills but also information about things like self-organization, diet, family planning, health and sustainable agriculture. Wan-gari Maathai, who is now working with the United Nations to establish similar programmes in several other African countries, has no doubt about either the importance of women in the future of her conti-nent or the intensely political nature of the Green Belt Movement:

The period for talking and complaining about the status of women was coming to an end and it appeared appropriate for women to talk around development issues and cause positive change in themselves, environment and country. Development issues provide a good forum for women to be creative, assertive and effective leaders and the Green Belt Movement, being a development issue, provided the forum to promote women's positive image.[9]

The green revolution is not, therefore, a brand new phenomenon thought up by hallucinating hippies in the 1960s. It is part of a historical trend. Nicholas Copernicus published his theory a good 200 years before its logical consequence (the industrial revolution) got into full swing. When we welcome the first year of the next century and the start of the next millennium it will be exactly 205 years after James Hutton published his theory that the world was one living system.

Furthermore, just as the political and economic systems which dominate the world today were shaped by men (sic) who were heavily influenced by the scientific and philosophical ideas of 100 or even 200 years ago, so current green notions about politics and economics are influenced by the scientific and philosophical notions advanced by Hutton, Lovelock and the atomic physicists. Therefore, far from being a random leap into the dark, any green future has a considerable body of knowledge and experience on which it can confidently build. Just as past agendas have been concerned to stitch together existing ideas into a coherent project for human beings, so the green agenda for the next century will be drawing on an ecological view of the world for its logic and coherence.

However, any agenda for the 21st century with the power to deliver a sustainable green future up to and beyond the end of the next millennium will have to be agreed upon and put into action within a decade. The speed at which our environment is losing its power to support life indicates that we do not have the luxury of another 100 years to get things right.

... Spiritually

For some considerable time, the stimuli which have turned our attention to the state of the environment have been negative ones. Although we still appreciate beautiful natural scenes on our calenders and TV screens or when we visit the countryside on holiday or at the weekend, nature remains peripheral to the 'real'-life, day-to-day experiences we have for most of the year. Indeed, for most people in densely populated Europe, those experiences take place in towns and cities, and when they do commune with nature it is mostly in managed parks rather than untamed wilderness.

The mounting pressure of what seem to be overwhelming environmental problems on governments, industry and ordinary people can, as I have already suggested, lead to an intensification of our 'flight or fight' reaction to threat and risk. It can also lead to a paralysis of the will and imagination, and I think it is this which is gripping many people at the moment. Old scientific certainties about how the physical world worked and old economic certainties about how unemployment levels, inflation and interest rates used to move in close relationship no longer underpin the experience of our governments. Old certainties about homes, jobs, pensions and convivial and safe communities in which to bring up children no longer underpin the experience of a growing number of ordinary people.

We are surrounded by crises – the environmental crisis, the economic crisis (recession), the crises in the Gulf and the Sudan, and the crises in the motor industry, education and the health service; the list seems endless. And as it grows longer and more complicated the persistent human dread of loss of control and failure looms larger. Not only has our idea about how the world ticks been proved faulty, but our faith in our own powers as a super-species in that world is being severely rattled. In many ways the biggest crisis we face is in our self-confidence.

For no doubt inscrutable reasons, the Chinese use the character *ji* to represent both crisis and opportunity. This double meaning in many ways sums up the turning-point at which we find ourselves as we enter the next century and start a new millennium. Either we sit in our armchairs and watch as a new dark age of increasing environmental degradation dawns, bringing with it incalcuble misery, or we seize the opportunity to get out of our armchairs, shake off the feeling that we can do nothing and apply our considerable brains and talents to turning the next era of history into a positive direction – towards a new enlightenment.

Chapter 3
Priorities For Action

> [The human predicament] is a spiritual predicament, for it requires us to be properly humble and grateful; time and again, it asks us to be still and wait. But it is also a practical problem, for it requires us to *do* things.

Wendell Berry, *The Landscape of Harmony*, 1987

The job of government is, of course, to govern, but we as citizens, especially those of us with access to some sort of democratic process, have a responsibility to make sure we get the sort of government we want. All our individual actions added up together may be the cause of global warming, loss of topsoil and so on, but they are actions which have been encouraged and rewarded by the political and economic systems we have favoured.

In our homes and at work, *doing* things in a greener way at the moment is either time-consuming, difficult, expensive or all three. Leaving the car in the garage and getting a bus would be fine if there were a decent public transport system. Taking papers and bottles to be recycled would be no trouble if the collection points were just down the road. Eating chemical-free food and insulating the loft would be wonderful if it didn't cost so much.

Therefore, although it is true that reversing environmental degradation will depend on changes in what we all do as individuals, a political and economic system which encourages and rewards green activity would make the world of difference. Without it, we may be able to do a bit, like using an environment-friendly washing powder or cleaning up some of the emissions from our factories, but we will never be able to do enough to make the changes called for by the reports I have mentioned in this book. The Global 2000 Report urged 'nations of the world [to] act decisively to alter current trends', while the Brundtland Report called for 'significant changes in current approaches'. Most recently the OECD has said: 'The key challenge for the 1990s is *to bring about cost-effective solutions to environmental problems through the structural adjustment of OECD economies.*' (OECD 1990, their emphasis)

So my agenda for a green 21st century concentrates on the decisive, significant and structural changes which will have to be made by governments if they and the global institutions to which they belong are to be a positive part of the green revolution rather than the agents which condemn us all to another dark age.

A Green agenda for the 21st century

1. To make a Historic Compromise between rich and poor.
2. To redefine security to mean the number of communities able to satisfy their needs near to where they are.
3. To transfer to an ecological economic system.
4. To move energy-use strategies out of the Fossil Fuel Age and into the Solar Age.
5. To expand rather than delimit wilderness.
6. To integrate human ecology with the ecology of nature.

Nevertheless, to set an agenda for governments is not to absolve ourselves from our responsibility as individual citizens. However nice it is to sit in our armchairs and point accusing fingers at politicians, bureaucrats, captains of industry, banks, churches, seats of learning and newspaper editors – all the people who 'run' society on our behalf – we are not really separate from them at all. By electing them, financing them with our taxes, buying their products, studying or worshipping at their knees or reading their books and papers we make ourselves responsible for the world they create. To paraphrase Tom Lehrer's ecological epigram: governments are like a sewer – what we get out of them depends on what we put into them.

1. The Historic Compromise

Since the collapse of the Warsaw Pact, there has been much talk of a 'new world order'. I find this term really rather sinister, because the old world order was the balance of power between the Communist bloc and the western alliance. As Dean and Clausen note, this required the participants to keep 'a total of 12 million men in arms and [consumed] about $600 billion a year, or two-thirds of the world's annual expenditure for armed forces'.[10] Therefore vague calls from US President George Bush and other world leaders for a *new* world order conjures up frightening visions of variations of the old one.

From a green point of view the 'world order' which matters more than any other is the one which will be discussed when every nation of the world meets in Brazil in June 1992. The UN Conference on Environment and Development has correctly identified the three most important international conventions which will have to be drawn up if the gravest threats to the life-sustaining powers of the environment are to be averted; if greenhouse gas emissions and the loss of both rainforest and biological diversity carry on unchecked, then irreparable damage (perhaps even in evolutionary terms) seems inevitable.

However, unless every signatory has a vested interest in making them come to life, these conventions, as any lawyer will explain, are in danger of becoming 'sleeping conventions' like many before them (CHEYNE in PARKIN 1991). Furthermore, unless they are underpinned by a radical reassessment of the relationship between rich and poor nations they are unlikely to be strong enough to meet even the most minimal targets in each area. Both poverty and affluence degrade the environment, but when it comes to the degradation of people, poverty wins hands down. Reversing both sorts of degradation will depend on active and willing participation from both rich and poor, but this will only be possible if the historic trend whereby today's poor countries effectively subsidize the lifestyle of the rich ones is reversed as well.

Therefore, at the top of any agenda concerned with greening the future, there must be a four-point agreement of principle – which I have called the Historic Compromise. This is an essential prelude to more detailed negotiations if global treaties on the environment are to avoid ending up in the pile of 'sleeping conventions'.

The Historic Compromise

1. All countries accept that we are (as a species) living beyond the means of the planet.
2. Rich countries accept that they must halt their development – which is here defined as the consumption of energy and raw materials.
3. Poor countries accept that they cannot pursue the same development patterns as the rich – in terms of the consumption of energy and raw materials.
4. Rich countries will start to pay back some of what they owe to the poor countries.

Point 4. is not a go-ahead for the poor and exploited to seek reparations for past injustices, however grave they may be. Indeed for some, like the wiping out of whole cultures, compensation is impossible. The Historic Compromise must be just that – a compromise, a truce on the past. This is explicit in point 1., which emphasizes that this is a *joint* project for all people. However, the transfer of cash, know-how, technology and so on implied in point 4. must be *entirely* adequate and appropriate to help the poor countries over current crises and onto a sustainable path. Experience so far makes it very clear that the details of this help are best designed and implemented by local communities rather than by international institutions or governments. (HARRISON 1987; TIMBER-LAKE & HOLMBERG 1991)

The close links of dependency between rich and poor countries are made clear in points 2. and 3. There is no way most rich countries can pursue their current activities without continued support from poor countries, either as sources of primary products or as places where waste can be disposed of. For example, the 12 Common Market countries are largely dependent on imports for primary products and currently produce around three times as much hazardous waste per year as the 'suitable facilities' for disposing of it within the Community can cope with.[11]

Likewise, there is no way poor countries can increase their consumption of energy and raw materials in emulation of the industrialized countries. For example, China currently produces some 9% of the world's carbon dioxide emissions from its coal burning. If, as Chinese energy analyst Professor Zhu Jiaheng anticipates, China depends on its large coal reserves to meet its plan to increase its energy demand six-fold by 2030, then what Dr Jeremy Leggett calls 'death-by-climate' for millions of people seems inescapable.[12]

Although, ecologically speaking, the balance of

power might be seen to tip in favour of poor countries which, despite their poverty, have theoretical control over the largest proportion of the world's biological resources, their rapidly growing populations and all-too-often corrupt and incompetent governments will tend to cancel out any advantage in practice. (EYRE 1978)

2. Redefining Security

One route by which governments may be hurried towards contemplating a Historic Compromise as a basis for any 'new world order' lies in the current debate about the future of NATO and other organizations which may or may not become involved in global security matters.

Recent events in eastern Europe have highlighted a conceptual problem behind the way words like 'threat', 'security' and 'defence' are used. Usually they are defined: loans are secured against default, for example, and windows are made secure against the threat of a storm. But in the hands of the military (and indeed the peace movement) it is assumed that these words need no definition: 'security forces in Europe', for example, means numbers of troops, not numbers of traffic police or environmental health officers. Defence budgets are spent on armies and navies, not on teams of people planting trees or grasses to prevent soil erosion.

This co-option of the notion of security by the military has blinkered us to the fact that although around 22 wars were fought in the last decade – more than in any previous decade in modern military history – they have not matched the scale of death and destruction due to environmental degradation.

Worldwide, a total of roughly 20 million people are thought to have died in armed conflict since 1945. Yet nowadays, around 20 million people are thought to die from hunger *every year*. The World Bank classifies 1 billion people, one fifth of humanity, as 'food insecure'. (WORLD BANK 1986)

Around half the world's population can be described as 'water insecure' – that is, they have inadequate access to safe drinking water and sanitary facilities or they depend on a shared river system to supply all their water needs. Disputes over water use and quality simmer in most regions of the world. About 20 million people live downstream of the heavily polluting industries of the Rhine, for example, and the flooding in the Ganges basin which regularly affects millions of people is greatly exacerbated by run-off and silting caused by deforestation in the distant Himalayas.[13]

Nowhere in the world is tension over water supplies more acute than in the Middle East. There 15 nations compete for the dwindling water reserves of the rivers Nile, Jordan and Euphrates. These rivers are all controlled by non-Arab states and conflicts abound. For example, Turkey is building a dam complex which could cut Syria's supplies from the Euphrates by half and Iraq's by two thirds.[14] A western diplomat in Damascus predicted in March 1990 (some time before Saddam Hussein invaded Kuwait) that the region was 'heading towards war, unless there is intervention by the United

Nations'.[15] And consider this excerpt from a public service advertisement inserted in the *Jerusalem Post* by the Israeli Minister of Agriculture on 18th August 1990 (*after* the invasion of Kuwait):

> The crucial issue to be considered in any political solution regarding the future of Judea and Samaria is the question of who will have the final authority in resolving issues in dispute. This is especially acute in the case of water resources, as any proposed Palestinian political entity, whether sovereign or autonomous, would have no water resources at all, other than those upon which Israel is so critically dependent for her day-to-day survival.

It seems strange, therefore, that when there is a discussion about security issues in the Middle East, water is rarely mentioned. Doubly strange when you consider that for the last eight years the biggest CIA research project has been on water security in that region.[16]

One of the consequences of war and political breakdown, of course, is that people tend to move. The United Nations Commission for Human Refugees estimates there to be around 15 million 'official' refugees and 'displaced persons', but these figures do not include those who have been forced to leave their homelands because of environmental degradation. Estimates here vary wildly from 10 million to 100 million people.

However, in the past we have seen the reluctance of governments to take even a small number of refugees. Moreover, during 1991 international relief budgets and personnel were stretched to the limit as vast numbers of Kurds fled the civil war in Iraq, millions tried to escape famine in Africa and millions more in Bangladesh tried to survive storms and floods. But these problems will be dwarfed by those which the warming of the planet will cause in the future. More harvests will fail and more sea-levels will rise, flooding coastlines where many human settlements are. Sea-water entering estuaries will salinate prime agricultural land and contaminate already diminished drinking water aquifers. Unprecedented numbers of people will be obliged to move.

For those of us living in the north of Europe, the idea of a warmer climate is perhaps rather appealing. However, the impact of global warming is, as the scientists emphasize, most likely to manifest itself in *unpredictable* climatic events (HOUGHTON et al 1990). Therefore, although there is no *proof* that they were linked to global warming, the storms which have hit the south of England in recent years are a sample of what we might expect.

In those storms roads and railway lines were blocked. Telephone and power lines were cut. Emergency services were stretched to their limits clearing away debris, providing supplies and coping with the ill and injured. Subsequently, insurance companies announced an increase in premiums because claims for storm damage and subsidence caused by summer droughts were so great. What will bigger storms and longer and more frequent droughts do to the cost and practicality of running emergency services? And at what point do insurance companies stop insuring against storm and drought damage?

So whether we consider human security in terms of the number of people already dead, or the numbers of people threatened with death, or the numbers of people obliged to leave their homeland because it can no longer support them, or even in terms of impact on our social and financial services, it would seem that the state of our environment poses a greater threat than any enemy army.

When people 'swarm' (i.e. move in large numbers, for whatever reason) they put huge environmental and social stresses on their host country, region or city, often extending misery all round and giving rise to dangerous resentment. This phenomenon is not limited to poor countries either. The very rapid unification of Germany was largely prompted by the spectre of huge numbers of eastern Europeans moving through a porous border into the creaking and costly welfare state of western Europe. Therefore very soon, we must stop thinking of human security in terms of divisions or battalions or warheads and think of it instead in terms of the number of communities able to satisfy their needs near to where they live, and therefore the number of people happy to stay at home.

3. Ecological Economics

Yet while the forecast is for famine, flood, pestilence and mounting human and environmental degradation, world military expenditure (all spent in the name of security) is running at around US$1,000 billion, roughly 10% of all world economic activity. The annual $100 billion military research and development budget is greater than all government research expenditure on developing new energy technologies, improving human health, increasing agricultural productivity and reducing birth rates *put together*.[17]

How has the way we spend our time, talents and money come to be so out of kilter with the real needs of people today? The reason is, inevitably, a complicated one with its roots deep in history. As Robert Heilbroner points out:

> The market system with its essential components of land, labour, and capital was . . . born in agony – an agony that began in the thirteenth century and had not run its course until well into the nineteenth. Never was a revolution less well understood, less welcomed, less planned.
> (HEILBRONER 1983)

However, what concerns us here is that the system which did evolve was enormously influenced by the 'marvellous science' of Descartes and his homologues. The term 'economics' (like 'ecology') comes from the Greek word *oikos*, meaning 'house'. Economics, therefore, should be all about good planetary housekeeping. But the urge to reduce everything to numbers meant that economists tended to marginalize anything which could not be represented in cash terms. To be fair, they recognized the perils of this from the beginning. Indeed, Adam Smith emphasized that the market was a dangerous force which had to operate within the restraining moral context of shared community values (DALY & COBB 1990). But the logical power to be found in the mechanical manipulation of numbers overwhelmed moral qualms again and again:

> ... the great market making forces could not be denied. Insidiously they ripped apart the mould of custom: insolently they tore away the usages of tradition ... The problem of survival was henceforth to be solved neither by custom nor by command, but by the free action of profit-seeking men bound together only by the market itself. The system was to be called capitalism. And the idea of gain which underlay it was to become so firmly rooted that men would soon vigorously affirm that it was an eternal and omni-present part of human nature.

(HEILBRONER 1978)

Gain, growth, expansion – these objectives govern household economies, national economies, the World Bank, the global markets – everything we do. In order to survive, to succeed, we must have *more* – more money, more things. Almost every country subscribes to this basic economic philosophy of more for *everybody*, and their various ideologies simply reflect different strategies for achieving this. The 'free-market' approach, for example, assumes that benefits from entrepreneurs will 'trickle down', while Communism assumes that everyone can gain at an equal rate if government plans it. There are, of course, many variations on these two basic themes, and arguments about which is the best dominate political discourse the world over.

However, Greens would argue that there are fatal

flaws in this economic system which cannot be resolved by tinkering with it. If we want a green future, then we will have to have a green economy as well – one which is considered successful if it provides *enough* for everyone, which rewards rather than penalizes compassion and justice between human beings, and which encourages the conservation of our environment rather than its consumption. As the diagram in Figure II shows, the theoretical shape of a green economy would be very different from the shape of the one we have at the moment. Moving from one to another and maintaining the green economy, however, would use all the usual economic instruments, like taxes, regulations, markets, well informed consumers and so on. Thus, while changing the shape of the economic regime which has governed the world for the last couple of years will indeed be a great challenge, it perhaps poses more of a psychological problem than a practical one.

In *For the Common Good* Herman Daly and John Cobb consider in some detail the philosophy and the mechanisms which would 'redirect the economy towards community, the environment and a sustainable future' (DALY 1990), while in *The Green Budget* David Kemball-Cook and his colleagues set out a self-financing budget for Britain which shows how the first steps towards a circular economy might be made. As they point out:

A green economy is one in which, whilst recognizing the necessary environmental constraints, ensures that fundamental needs are met equitably throughout the world. This means that any

The "Consumer" Economic Model (linear – unsustainable)

To succeed (grow, expand):	Must do more of all this.
Human well-being:	Equated with quantity of product.
Assumption:	If quantity of product increasing, then well-being OK.
Main indicator:	Gross National Product.
To be more efficient:	Participants must "externalize" as many costs as possible.
Dynamic:	Towards the largest economic theatre (market) possible – globalizing.
Features:	Centralized, highly automated (energy-intensive) production. Uni- or low-skilled workforce.

The "Conserver" or "Green" Economic Model (circular – sustainable)

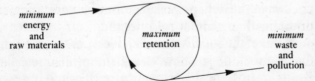

To succeed (grow, expand):	Must do more of all this.
Human well-being:	Equated with quality of life.
Assumption:	If well-being improving, then production OK.
Main indicator(s):	Basket of economic, social and environmental indicators.
To be more efficient:	Participants must 'internalize' as many costs as possible.
Dynamic:	Towards the smallest economic theatre (market) possible – localizing.
Features:	Diverse, local, human-based (energy-efficient) production. Flexibly skilled workforce.

production system must be based not only on minimum input, maximum retention and minimum output, but also on respect for the dignity of people.[18]

It is therefore not an accident that most green economists consider the starting-point of any transition to an ecological economic system to be the adoption of more realistic methods of measuring human well-being. The current favourite indicator, gross national product (GNP), was never meant to be more than that – a gross measure of the product of an economy. It was definitely not intended to double up as an indicator (gross or otherwise) of human well-being. Its principal merit is that it is a number, and therefore understandable to traditionally trained economists.

In a green economy, human well-being would be measured by a basket of indicators (not all numerical) which would include environmental ones, like the quality of air, food and water and the number of species, and also social ones, like equity ratios, health statistics and crime rates – even neighbourhood 'conviviality' (safety, closeness of schools, shops etc.) could be included. The point is that while a standard basket might exist for comparison, the contents of the basket could vary from community to community, could be decided by the community itself and could be adjusted as goals and possibilities changed. A green economist would be someone with wide experience in many fields, and the discipline of economics would be transformed from a 'dismal science' to a high art form.

The meeting of the world's governments in Brazil in 1992 offers a golden opportunity for them to decide to use a wide-ranging basket of indicators parallel with and therefore comparable to GNP. Moving from consumer-driven to a green conserver-driven economy will depend on many changes in every area of economic activity of course. But publishing a set of *real-life* indicators would do a great deal to set in motion changes in other sectors of the economy. Most of the indicators which a greening economy would use are already available, but governments have so far proved reluctant to publish them in a way which invites comparison with the usual economic ones. (ANDERSON 1991; OECD 1990)

Once economies (and just as importantly, the people living and working in them) can see an alternative to GNP, new accounting methods can then remove the crazy anomalies that presently exist. For example, when the Exxon Valdez spilt its oil in Prince William Sound, the coastline and the wildlife of Alaska were devastated and the local fishing industry was ruined. Yet the economy of Alaska recorded a boom year, because the millions of dollars spent on trying to clean up the coast were entered as a credit in the state's accounts. Similarly, the money a community spends on treating sick people or dealing with crime is put through on the positive side of the accounts. On the other hand, planting trees or buying energy efficiency is recorded as a cost.

If the goal of an economy is not simply to maximize the activity of cash, but to improve human and environmental health, then in the time it takes to turn a page of a ledger, accountants will see the sense of entering the figures in different columns. This would give the logic of the conserver economy a chance to become more powerful than that of the linear economy, and would enable the transition to an ecological and therefore sustainable system to take on a momentum of its own.

4. Out of the Fossil Fuel Age and Into the Solar Age

One of the economists who inspires Greens is Nicholas Georgescu-Roegen. He describes himself as a 'bioeconomist' and argues that we should account for our activities biologically. As long as we produce bigger, better and more things like washing machines, cars and airplanes, he says, then we are automatically going to produce bigger, better and more pollution. Only by cutting back on the amount of raw materials and energy which goes *through* our economy will we be able to reduce the pollution which comes out the other end. Georgescu-Roegen considers that our economic theory should be based on the scientific laws of thermodynamics, which are concerned with energy transformations. (GEORGESCU-ROEGEN 1971)

Robert Mueller, from the Planetology Branch of Goddard Space Flight Center (NASA), has come to the same conclusion:

The technology of man may be regarded as a heat engine and as such is subject to thermodynamic principles which govern energy transformations. In this context pollution in its myriad forms is seen as the agent by which the total energy input is dissipated into the environment.[19]

For governments to feel that an economy is performing adequately, it has to grow at a rate of about 3% per year. However, as things are at the moment, this growth implies a *doubling* of consumption every 25 years with, of course, a concomitant increase in pollution (EKINS 1986). It is certainly possible to change these ratios. More efficient use of resources and energy would indeed lengthen the consumption-doubling time and lower the amount of pollution. But the economy would still be in the linear consumer mode, so, because of its dynamic and its definition of success, it would still have to go on chomping its way through the environment at an ever-increasing rate.

Moving our economies into a conserver, circular mode would largely resolve this crucial problem. Its dynamic and its definition of success would mean the through-put of raw material and energy would be increasingly reduced.

But while moving whole economies from the linear to the circular mode might be planned over three or more decades, the climate scientists are urging an *immediate* cut of *at least* 60% in emissions of carbon-dioxide (the main greenhouse gas) if we are to have a reasonable chance of averting global warming.

As both the bioeconomists and space scientists like Lovelock and Mueller confirm, radically reducing the amount of carbon dioxide coming *out* of our economies means radically reducing the amount of energy going *in*. Although governments at present are wringing their hands over this and taking very little action, all the technology and know-how to meet the demands of the climate scientists actually exists already.

Amory Lovins of the Rocky Mountain Institute considers the potential of energy efficiency alone to be such that 'it is generally cheaper today to save fuel than to burn it. Avoiding pollution by not burning the fuel, can, therefore, be achieved, not at a cost, but at a profit – so this result can and should be widely implemented in the market-place.' Lovins is convinced that, even with the economy still in linear mode,

> [an] 'efficiency scenario', assuming the same economic and population growth but using energy in a way that saves money (under 1980 conditions, which are probably less favourable than today's), uses four to five times less energy, costs much less, stretches oil and gas for centuries, dispenses with reliance on both the Middle East and the atom, and by 2030 has attained an atmospheric CO_2 level barely above today's.

If this is possible, why are governments not doing it? Lovins suspects that what he calls 'corporate socialism' is to blame: governments protect their favourite technologies, even though many of them, like the nuclear industry, are now dying of an incurable attack of market forces (LOVINS in LEGGETT 1990). If you consider that the UK government annually invests £159 million in its nuclear programme compared to £17 million in its renewable sources of energy programme, and has actually *cut back* on its already measly energy efficiency programme, then you are forced to agree.

However, the dynamic against reducing energy through-put in the linear economy runs deeper than that. Global markets do not encourage companies either to seriously economize on energy or to transfer any 'state-of-the-art' technologies to potential competitors. For example, General Electric have set up a $150 million project to modernize 13 Hungarian light-bulb factories. If instead they had used the money to move manufacture to energy-efficient compact fluorescent bulbs (the use of which reduces demand for electricity), the Hungarian government could have saved $10,000 million in the construction of new coal-fired power plants.[20] Only if the dynamic of the economy is directed towards minimal energy input and the diversification of local markets can energy efficiency truly come into its own.

The same goes for renewable sources of energy. Until the tax system and other economic incentives prioritise them, they will remain the Cinderellas of energy provision, in the shadow of their big polluting ugly sisters, coal, oil, gas and the atom.

And yet it is only by trimming our energy-use sails until we can live within the annual energy budget of the sun that we can be confident of a truly sustainable green future. However we manage to eke them out or use them more cleanly, fossil fuels are polluting and in finite supply; we count the time until they are exhausted in decades. At 1988 rates of use we have around 150 decades of coal left, 12 decades of natural gas and around 6 decades of oil.[21] Even if we manage to double or even triple our efficiency in using them, that is hardly enough to see a rising world population through a third millennium. By contrast, the sun delivers the energy equivalent of about 60,000 billion metric tons of oils *each year* and will go on doing so until it finally burns itself out – a moment thought to be many millions of millennia in the future. (LEAN 1990)

The possibilities for capturing solar radiation directly to make thermal energy or electricity or indirectly through biomass, wind and hydro-technologies are immense, and despite the pitifully meagre investment in renewable energy sources, the costs are tumbling. For example, the Danish Ministry of Energy reports that electricity from wind-power costs just 5.3 cents per kilowatt hour (kWh) and electricity from biomass costs about 5 cents per kWh. This compares well with coal at around 3 cents per kWh and very well with nuclear power at 13 cents per kWh (the current cost in Britain and the USA). (LAPORTA and KEEPIN in LEGGETT 1990)

Even the cost of photovoltaic cells, which have been described as the 'quintessential' method of transforming solar energy, has tumbled from $1 per kWh to around 25 cents per kWh in a decade. They are already being used cost-effectively in remote areas such as the Australian outback. They create electricity with no pollution, no noise and often no moving parts. They need no water and little maintenance, and can operate on any scale. Because they can be fitted to any roof in the world, however remote, photovoltaic cells are certain to play a crucial role not only in reducing the through-put of energy in any economy, but also in the democratization of energy use as both rich and poor countries move towards low-energy-use strategies.[22]

Moving into the Solar Age will be a momentous step for humankind. But it is an urgently needed one, and the sooner government investment and planning reflect this the better.

5. Expanding Wilderness

Thinking about the world ecologically and considering the links that exist between all life on earth has highlighted just how many of those links are being broken. No one really knows how many species of plants, animals and micro-organisms there are in the world, and estimates vary wildly between 5 million and 30 million. We do know that we have identified and named only about 1.4 million of them. We also know that during the 4 billion years since life first appeared on earth it has been normal for some species to become naturally extinct. However, the current rate of species extinction is running at around 25,000 times the natural rate. (LEAN 1990; WWF 1989)

The primary cause of this loss of species is the activities of a rapidly expanding human population; it is thought that we already monopolize around 40% of the net primary (biological) production of the earth. Some species like whales and fish, are being threatened because we are over-hunting them, but the biggest danger to species is the loss of habitat, either through destruction or severe degradation.

If (and all the evidence we have points to this) life on earth is entirely dependent on the vastly complicated relationship between all these millions of species, then keeping up our current rate of destroying them is an act of collective suicide. As the Worldwide Fund for Nature points out:

> The diverse living components of dynamic ecosystems give them a certain stability. But even ecosystems interact. Terrestrial ecosystems recycle water, but also absorb it from storms which gather over the oceans. The excess drains from the land as rivers, taking with it nutrients which enrich the shallow seas of the continental shelf. Countless processes of this nature make the biosphere a self-regulating system ensuring the continuity of life.

The need to conserve species and their habitats is not only a practical one, to do with our own survival as a species; it is also an ethical one. The tropical rainforests, for example, which cover only 14% of the world's land surface yet hold at least half the world's species, are more than just a source of medicines, food and climatic stabilizers for human beings; they are the source of life for many other species too. If we human beings are intent on self-destruction, which right do we have to condemn other species to the same fate?

So far, our efforts to protect biodiversity have been miserable. Less than 3% of the world's land surface is covered by nature reserves, national parks or wildlife sanctuaries, and the rate of species and habitat loss goes on increasing. However, as long as there is a straight competition between current notions of economic efficiency and the environment, then it will be the latter which will lose. Witness the recent decision by Prime Minister Bob Hawke to renege on his election pledges to the powerful Australian green movement in favour of legislation which will guarantee the timber industry access to once-protected forest.[23]

We need to expand our wildernesses, not squeeze them into 'ghettos' or treat them like museums. They are the heart, lungs and mind of the living world to which we belong. As Bob Brown, one of the most consistent and courageous defenders of the Australian wilderness puts it:

> Our bodies and minds are made for wildness. Through millions of years, every human cell has been created and made ready for the Earth's terrain. The spread of our toes, the grip of our hands, the curl of our ears to catch the faintest movements of air molecules by fur, feather or fin: billions of wilderness cells making us up.[24]

So, instead of putting fences around the wildernesses or organizing them into parks, we should make expanding them a top priority for a green future. Practically speaking, we need them to be back in full control of the regulating mechanisms of the biosphere. Ethically, we need to make the connection between ourselves and all life if we are to be able to live our lives in a way which conserves rather than consumes the world around us.

6. Human Ecology

Finding a way to live within the ecological constraints of the biosphere is ultimately a human project. It is our activities which we have to manage in a different way, not the activities of the biosphere. It has billions of years of experience of organizing ecological balance, and it is not known for compassion towards any species which steps out of line.

Working out the details of what a green society might look like and how to get there is of vital importance, and as someone who has written programmes for more than one election campaign, I do have quite strong views on what a lot of those details might be. But as with the rest of my agenda for the 21st century, I want to stick to the headlines – the most essential points which will have to be addressed if the other more detailed ones are ever to see the light of day. In any green future, it is the principles which matter; details are always negotiable.

I therefore want to concentrate on the two features of how we human beings operate our ecology which need the most urgent action. The first is our absolute numbers, because, however much we cut down our individual impact on the planet, there is an inevitable limit to the number of people the biosphere can support. The second is the need for us to reconsider the way we have drawn the political map of the world. This has given us a set of national and institutional boundaries which are rather different from the boundaries of the problems we have to tackle

– a real handicap to our search for solutions.

If we want to use choice rather than catastrophe as the mechanism which will bring our numbers into balance with the world's carrying capacity, we will have to act fast. And, even though rates of growth are much greater for poor countries, this is definitely a project for both rich and poor. The rich countries of the European Community (EC), for example, form one of the most densely populated regions of the world, so without the environmental services (i.e. primary products and pollution sinks) of countries other than their own, they would certainly be suffering from 'Third World' problems like cholera and famine. However, as most of the countries on which the EC depends are increasingly struggling with growing populations, a rapidly degrading environment and all the human misery that goes with those problems, it is not sure for how much longer it can rely on these services. Faced with the growing anger of their own hungry people and the EC's wish to buy in grain for its livestock or to sell off its cars, the governments of poor countries are beginning to realize that charity must begin at home. Mrs Maneka Gandhi, former Environment Minister of India, a country with a rapidly growing population, has quite bluntly posed the question: 'What will happen if we [meaning the Third World] agree sanctions towards you?'[25]

It is perhaps premature to put an 'ideal number' on what the carrying capacity of any particular world region might be, but considering it should be a regular topic of public debate. The first job is to slow and then halt the current rate of population growth world-wide. And although the rich countries have more or less done this already, because they consume such a disproportionate amount of the world's primary resources and create the bulk of the world's pollution, they must move at once to reduce their numbers.

Giving women confidence that the children they give birth to will survive in health and well-being into adulthood must be at the heart of any programme to reduce human numbers. Again this goes for both rich and poor countries. Cancer specialists note that 'population comparisons and evidence from experimental and epidemiological studies strongly suggest that as much as 80–90% of human cancer is determined environmentally and thus theoretically avoidable'.[26] They also note:

> the preponderance of chemicals among the human carcinogens appears clearly to be related to industrial development, and in particular that of the chemical industry which began in the second half of the last century and has grown steadily ever since ... Industrial development took place initially with little if any concern for possible health effects. This was due partly to genuine ignorance, especially about long-term adverse effects such as cancer; later, however, adverse health effects were dismissed, either as unavoidable evils or as of too little importance to justify expensive modifications to production procedures.[27]

On a world scale, cancer is the third most common cause of death, but it is predominantly a disease of rich countries. For the poor, infection and parasitic diseases exacerbated by malnutrition top the league by a long chalk. Therefore, giving women everywhere the power, in the shape of information *and* practical support, to provide a healthy environment for their children is essential if they are to have enough confidence to have fewer children.

It is also time for world religious leaders to consider carefully how they preach their gospels. The Koran, for example, places a 'divine responsibility' on parents to provide for their children. But in many Moslem countries families of about six are common and both infant and maternal mortality rates are high. This suggests that responsibility is not divine enough to provide sufficiently for the basic needs and rights of women which is essential if the well-being of their children is to be safeguarded. From a Catholic point of view, Sean McDonagh argues that being pro-life has to have a much broader meaning than being pro- the birth of more and more babies. As UNICEF points out, *every week* more than a quarter of a million children are born only to be condemned to death from malnutrition or easily preventable diseases. Yet neither Pope John Paul's famous pro-life encyclical *Humanae Vitae* nor any subsequent document from the Catholic Church has contemplated the fact that defending human life in a narrow way may ultimately endanger all life on earth.
(McDONAGH 1990; UNICEF 1990)

But while cultural and economic changes are essential for a sustained and voluntary reduction in the number of births, the most urgent need is to get information and materials to women to help them prevent the conception of unplanned children. According to the UN World Fertility Survey most women, even in the poorest of countries, know about some method of contraception or other. After all, throughout history women have sought ways of controlling their own fertility. In Cleopatra's Egypt, for example, using the peel of half an orange was a favourite method; it was worn like a modern rubber contraceptive cap, and its acidity worked as a spermicide.

The same survey also showed that a majority of women who wanted contraceptive advice and materials couldn't get them. Meeting this need, and giving the women who already want to limit their fertility the power to do so, would make a massive difference to birth rates in a relatively short period of time. Similarly, in rich countries a significant proportion of conceptions, both in and out of marriage, are unwelcome. By preventing these and by providing plenty of information about the links between a personal decision to have a child and our global responsibilities, population levels could be brought down reasonably quickly.

The Gulf War demonstrated how precision bombing makes it possible for the military to respect the integrity of the nation state. However, the plight of the Kurds has subsequently emphasised that the notion of political boundaries is meaningless to starving and frightened people. Acid rain, nuclear fall-out, droughts and floods have always paid more respect to geography and climate than to customs posts.

The accident at Chernobyl, the Gulf War and the present strategic dilemmas of both NATO and the European Community all remind us that the boundaries of our problems and the fora in which we try to work out the solutions all too often do not fit together.

The classic example is to be found in the serious tensions inside the EC. Doubts and arguments about the European 1992 project are, in fact, so severe that they have already caused the downfall of two prime ministers: Margaret Thatcher of Britain and Michel Rocard of France. The source of the problem is that, since the 1987 Single European Act, the EC has found itself with two *incompatible* goals. The original objective of creating a barrier-free internal market has been joined by a second – to make the EC into a trading block strong enough to compete with Japan and America.

Unfortunately the sort of policies which will create an internal market offering reasonably equal benefits to all its members are quite the opposite to those which will render the EC a lean, mean competitor in the world markets. The discovery that the interests of European regions and the interests of the world market are in tune neither with each other nor with what are currently perceived to be 'national interests' lies at the heart of the current debate about Europe.

Moreover, despite evidence from the Roman Empire to the Russian Empire that detailed organizing on such a scale is unsustainable, the debate about Europe has largely focussed on political and economic minutia. It has certainly failed to take into account the overriding problem of a rapidly degrading environment – the sole topic of the '*other* 1992' which will be taking place in Brazil. A report on the EC's 1992 and its environmental impact, prepared for the European Commission, warned of the dangers of neglecting the environment: 'it cannot be assumed that the removal of barriers within the Community will automatically of itself give rise to the most beneficial outcome for the Community and its citizens'.[28]

Getting the boundaries within which we can resolve our problems to match the boundaries in which the problems present themselves must be a top priority for bodies like the European Council of Ministers, NATO and the United Nations. And liberating ourselves from thinking only in terms of the current political boundaries is as good a place to start as any. After all, the idea of the nation state is a fairly new one, only dating back to around 1789. The United Nations and NATO are not yet 50 years old and the European Community is under 35. Given the magnitude and urgency of the problems to be tackled and the desire for sustainability to be counted in thousands of years rather than decades, then rethinking our institutions is surely worthwhile.

Something which has a much longer history than the nation state is the ecological fact that the stability of any system depends on the various parts of the system fulfilling their functions satisfactorily. Individual cells, for example, are very different from the whole organism, but while the body may dominate cell formation (and so decide the ultimate shape and function of the whole), it is in turn dependent on the cells staying alive and well.

In the realm of human organisation, this arrangement – where every part of life is interdependent but has a clear role in the organization of the body (or biosphere) – is *partly* translated into the principle of *subsidiarity*. (Greens would argue that the complexity of the arrangement is too often neglected.)

This principle was famously defined in a papal encyclical as follows:

> It is an injustice and at the same time a grave evil and disturbance of right order to assign to a greater and higher association what lesser and subordinate organizations can do. For every social activity ought of its very nature to furnish help to the members of the body social and never destroy and absorb them.[29]

What this boils down to is that decisions should be taken at the smallest appropriate level, and cooperation rather than competition should govern relationships between all levels. Using the principle of subsidiarity to help us choose our institutions for the future would provide coherence where at present there is chaos. For example, a Europe of Regions, where the regions were more defined by biological features like seas, mountains and river basins, would not only make a lot of sense but would also build on what is happening already around the North Sea and the Mediterranean, in the Nordic Region and the High Alps, along the Danube and so on. Italy's Foreign Minister has even floated the idea of a Conference on Security and Cooperation in the Mediterranean which would include North Africa and the Middle East. The principle of subsidiarity also moves with the growing demand for more local autonomy coming from all over the world: from, for example, Kurdistan, Palestine, Croatia, the Baltic States, Scotland, Northern Italy and the Basque country.

This trend – to move the functional units of human organization downwards towards smaller sub-national regions with a cultural and geographical affinity and upwards towards international groupings prompted by common environmental concerns – is an important one, and the governments meeting in Brazil would be foolish to ignore it.

Working with it and taking particular care to get the right sort of decision made at the right level would not only provide a more coherent framework for policy development in Europe and other world regions, but would also give badly needed substance to any notion of a new world order. If, for example, global fora like the Brazil Conference or the United Nations and world regional fora like the 34-nation Conference on Security and Cooperation in Europe, the South Pacific Forum or the Organization of African Unity were to concentrate on establishing a new ethic for international relations (based on, say, the Historic Compromize), setting global targets for things like greenhouse gas emissions or land reclamation and agreeing new indicators of human well-being, then national and sub-national groupings could concentrate on the practical steps needed to meet those targets.

Getting the principles right at the international level and leaving the practical details to the local level would give the human project a much better chance of achieving its goals than would the present system. This is now so bogged down in conflicts

over details at the international level that it has
largely abandoned principles at all levels.

Right Relationships

> The crux of the matter is not only whether the human species will survive, but even more whether it can survive without falling into a state of worthless existence. (MEADOWS et al. 1972)

These closing words from *Limits of Growth* sum up the predicament which faces us. Old certainties are breaking down – scientific ones, political ones, personal ones. The whiff of fear of chaos is as much abroad in Washington as it is in Moscow as the bizarre balance of power which we took to be world stability disappears, taking with it the logical pot of glue which made sense of the world.

The triumphalism which accompanied the final admission that Communism was bankrupt covered up the increasing 'uneconomic growth' in the rest of the world. Our horror at seeing the massive pollution in eastern Europe made us forget the constraints which the state of the environment had put on our own economies. For example, as the

Berlin Wall came down, so did the Dutch government – over an Environment Plan for the densely
populated and heavily polluted Netherlands.[30]
Commenting on the enormous pressures being put
on eastern European governments to emulate the
economic strategies of the west, one environment
minister from the east has said: 'We are in danger
of swapping our old-fashioned environmental and
economic problems for your modern ones.'

Times of uncertainty and fear of chaos are also
times of danger. History is littered with examples
of how chaos benefits the baddies much more than
the goodies. Mussolini himself pointed out that
'fascism was not the nurseling of a doctrine worked
out beforehand in detailed elaboration; it was born
of the need for action'.[31] Which is why I have
concentrated in this book on the philosophy and
the principles of ecological thinking. I fear there is
a real danger that in the search for a new pot of
glue with which to make sense of the world around
them – something which will provide both a
psychological and a political focus – people and
their governments will move towards the *simplicity*
of repressive and fanatical doctrines. The tendency
is evident in too many countries already. It would
be so easy for any organization which took on
responsibility for Europe's security to slip into the
simple new certainty of Christians versus Islam, for
example, or for the 'new world order' to sink into
a dark age of resource wars and feuding regions.

When speaking of negotiations over Europe, or
of the unresolved crisis in the Gulf, politicians
frequently speak of taking matters 'step by step'.
What they try to promote as mature and responsible

statesmanship is nothing but a cover for their bank-ruptcy of imagination – their lack of vision. So absorbed are they in their detailed steps that they cannot see the abyss towards which they are heading.

By taking a *green* look at human history we can gain a new perspective on the past and a new confidence that there is a vision for the future with *limitless* possibilities. However, it is also clear that a green future cannot be bought on the world market, nor can it be forced upon an unwilling and uncomprehending people. It can only be secured through personal and political choice.

In my agenda for the 21st century I have tried to show that new perspective and some of the possi-bilities it illuminates. I believe that it is the only logical pot of glue which will be strong enough to unite the world around the urgent task of securing a life-supporting environment. Carrying out that task will not be simple, that is for sure, but it must be carried out if humankind is to have a long-term future. I made my personal and political choices a while ago, and despite the enormity of the task, it still feels more like a great opportunity than a ter-minal crisis.

How the 21st century unfolds for my children and for the rest of their generation depends on how many other people come to the same conclusion – and how quickly.

At the moment our epitaph is being drafted. It reads: 'They saw it coming but hadn't the wit to avoid it.' I am confident that there is still time to intervene and *do something*, so the end of the human story may be rewritten like this: 'They saw it coming, but acted with ecological wisdom, and so lived happily ever after.'

A thing is right when it tends to preserve the integrity, stability and beauty of the biotic community. It is wrong when it tends otherwise.

Aldo Leopold, *A Sand County Almanac*, 1948

Bibliography

Anderson, Victor, *Alternative Economic Indicators*, Routledge, London, 1991.

Berry, Wendell, *The Landscape of Harmony*, Five Seasons Press, Hereford, 1987.

Brown, Lester, et al., *State of the World*, W. W. Norton, New York, 1989.

Brown, Lester, et al., *State of the World*, W. W. Norton, New York, 1990.

(Brundtland Report) World Commission on Environment and Development, *Our Common Future*, Oxford University Press, Oxford, 1987.

Capra, Fritjof, *The Turning Point*, Wildwood House, London, 1982.

Carson, Rachael, *Silent Spring*, Houghton Mifflin, Boston, 1962, reissued 1987.

The Ecologist, A Blueprint for Survival, Penguin, Harmondsworth, 1972.

Ekins, Paul (ed.), *The Living Economy*, Routledge & Kegan Paul, London, 1986.

Eyre, R. S., *The Real Wealth of Nations*, Edward Arnold, London, 1978.

Daly, H. & Cobb, J., *For the Common Good*, Greenprint, London, 1989.

Erlich, P. & Erlich, A., *Earth*, Methuen, London, 1987.

Erlich, P. & Erlich, A., *The Population Explosion*, Methuen, London, 1990.

George, Susan, *A Fate Worse than Debt*, Penguin, Harmondsworth, 1988.

Georgescu-Roegen, Nicholas, *The Entropy Law and the Economic Process*, Harvard University Press, Cambridge, Massachusetts, 1971.

(Global 2000 Report) The Council on Environmental Quality and the Department of State, *The Global 2000 Report to the President: Entering the Twenty-first Century*, Penguin, Harmondsworth, 1982.

Harrison, Paul, *The Greening of Africa*, Paladin, London, 1987.

Heilbroner, Robert, *The Worldly Philosophers*, Penguin, Harmondsworth, 1983.

Houghton, J. T., Jenkins, G. J. & Ephrams, J. J. (eds.), *Climate Change: The IPCC Scientific Assessment, Report to IPCC from Working Group 1*, World Meteorological Organisation, UNEP, Cambridge University Press, Cambridge, 1990.

Hutton, J., *Theory of the Earth with Proofs and Illustrations*, William Creech, Edinburgh, 1795.

Kemball-Cook, D., Baker, M. & Mattingly, C. (eds.), *The Green Budget*, Green Print, London, 1991.

Lean, Geoffrey (ed.), *Atlas of the Environment*, Arrow Books, London, 1990.

Leggett, Jeremy (ed.), *Global Warming: The Greenpeace Report*, Oxford University Press, Oxford, 1990.

Leopold, Aldo, *A Sand County Almanac*, Oxford Univeristy Press, New York, 1948.

Lovelock, James, *Gaia: A New Look at Life on Earth*, Oxford University Press, Oxford, 1979.

McCormick, John, *The Global Environment Movement*, Belhaven Press, London, 1989.

McDonagh, Sean, *To Care for the Earth*, Geoffrey Chapman, London, 1986.

McDonagh, Sean, *The Greening of the Church*, Geoffrey Chapman, London, 1990.

McIntyre, A., *A Short History of Ethics*, Routledge & Kegan Paul, London, 1967.

Meadows, D., et al., *The Limits to Growth*, Earth Island, London, 1972.

Parkin, Sara, *Green Parties: An International Guide*, Heretic, London, 1989.

Parkin, Sara (ed.), *Green Light on Europe*, Heretic, London, 1991.

Schumacher, E. F., *Small is Beautiful*, Abacus, London, 1973.

Timberlake, L. & Holmberg, J., *Defending the Future: A Guide to Sustainable Development*, Earthscan, London, 1991.

Organization for Economic Co-operation and Development, *The State of the Environment*, Paris, 1991.

Organization for Economic Co-operation and Development, *Environmental Indicators*, Paris, 1990.

United Nations Environment Programme, *Environmental Data Report*, Basil Blackwell, Oxford, 1989/90.

World Bank, *Poverty and Hunger*, Washington DC, 1986.

Worldwide Fund for Nature, *The Importance of Biological Diversity*, Gland, 1989.

References

1. Revelations, Chapter xx, v 7–8
2. Roberts, J. M. (1980) *History of the World*, Penguin, Harmondsworth
3. Marsh, G. P. (1874) *Man and Nature* quoted in Wilman Ingela, M. B. *Expecting the Unexpected: Some Ancient Roots to Current Perceptions of Nation*, *Ambio*, Vol 19, No 2, April 1990
4. Cicero, *Nature of Gods*, ii 60, quoted in Wilman (see endnote 3)
5. Capra, Fritjof (1982) *The Turning Point*, Wildwood House, London
6. Merchant, Caroline (1980) *Death of Nature*, Harper & Row, New York
7. Food and Agriculture Organisation, Press Release PR 91/27
8. *Declaration of the UN Conference on the Human Environment*, June 1972, UNEP
9. Maathai, Wangari, *Building Blocks for Sustainable Development*, paper for The Other Economic Summit, London, June 1985
10. Dean J., Clausen, P. (1988) *The INF Treaty and*

the Future of Western Security, Union of Concerned Scientists, Cambridge, Massachusetts

11. European Commission (1987) *The European Community and the Environment*, Periodical 3/1987, EC, Luxembourg

12. Leggett, Jeremy, *Coal in Chinese Energy Consumption Plans: Implications for Global Warming Policy in Developed Countries*, no date, Greenpeace, London

13. Myers, Norman, *Environment and Security*, *Foreign Policy* 74, Spring 1989

14 Prins, Gwyn & Stamp, Robert (1991) *Top Guns and Toxic Whales*, Earthscan, London

15. Christian Science Monitor, 8/13/14/16, March 1990

16. See for example Starr, R. J. and Stoll, D. C. (eds.) (1988) *The Politics of Scarcity: Water in the Middle East*, Westview Press, Boulder, Colorado

17. Renner, Michael, *National Security: The Economic and Environmental Dimensions*, Worldwatch Paper 98, May 1989

18. Kemball-Cook, David, et al. (1991) *The Green Budget*, Green Print, London

19. Mueller, Robert, *Thermodynamics of Environmental Degradation*, paper presented at the Annual Meeting of the American Geophysical Union, March 1971, Washington

20. French, Marcia, *Green Revolutions: Environmental Reconstruction in Eastern Europe and the Soviet Union*, Worldwatch Paper 99, November 1990

21. Fulkerson, William, et al., *Energy from Fossil Fuels*, *Scientific American*, Vol 263, No 3, September 1990

22. Weinberg, C. J. & Williams, R. H. *Energy from the Sun*, *Scientific American*, Vol 263, No 3, September 1990

23. *The Australian, PM forsakes Greens in drive for Industry*, 7 March 1991

24. Brown, Bob, *Greening the Conservation Movement* in Hutton, Drew (ed.) (1987) *Green Politics in Australia*, Angus and Robertson, London
25. Debate at the Oxford Union, February 1991
26. Muir, C. S. & Parkin, D. M., *The World Cancer Burden: prevent or perish*, *British Medical Journal*, 5 January 1985, 290 5–6
27. Tomatis, L. (editor in chief) (1990) *Cancer: Causes, Occurrence and Control*, IARC Scientific Publications, No 100, Lyon
28. Task Force Report on the Environment and the Internal Market (199) *'1992': The Environmental Dimension*, Commission of the European Communities, Luxembourg
29. *Quadragesimo Anno*, papal encyclical
30. RIVM (1989) *Concern for Tomorrow*, National Institute of Public Health and Environment Protection, Bilhoven
31. Quoted in Palmer, R. R. & Colton, J. (1971) *A History of the Modern World since 1815*, Knopf, New York